The Seven Whispers

By the author

Life s Companion: Journal Writing as a Spiritual Quest

Calling the Circle: the First and Future Culture

The Seven Whispers

Listening to the Voice of Spirit

Christina Baldwin

New World Library
Novato, California

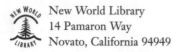 New World Library
14 Pamaron Way
Novato, California 94949

Cover design: Alexandra Graham
Text design and layout: Tona Pearce Myers

Library of Congress Cataloging-in-Publication Data
Baldwin, Christina.
The seven whispers : listening to the voice of spirit / Christina Baldwin.
    p.   cm.
ISBN 1-57731-192-2 (alk. paper)
1. Spiritual life. I. Title.
BL624 .B345 2002
291.4'4—dc21   2001005839

First printing, February 2002
ISBN 1-57731-192-2
Printed in Canada on acid-free, partially recycled paper
Distributed to the trade by Publishers Group West

10 9 8 7 6 5 4 3 2 1

To Ann—
oh joyful adventure

✣ Contents

❧ Introduction: A Spiritual Practice for Times like These

Prayer is not a pious gesture at all.
It is a response to the One whose heart beats with ours.

Joan Chitester

I love you, I love you.
That is all that has ever mattered.
Live your full life and I will always be with you.

Cell phone call, September 11, 2001

I have believed all my life that there is a necessary interaction that occurs between a person and the Divine. This interaction does not come only to prophets, bodhisattvas, and other great spiritual masters, it comes also to us: ordinary people in our ordinary lives. It is part of our natural human capacity to call out one of the thousand names of "God." And it is part of our human capacity to perceive and interpret the response.

Call and response is perhaps the oldest impulse we know. Humankind has always looked up and bowed down before the mysteries of the universe and asked God to become present. Moses, Buddha, Jesus, Mohammed — religions arise from a lineage of trembling prophets who understood that, if summoned, God might actually appear. Their stories say these were ordinary men and women who were pulled out of their ordinary lives into the service of what they summoned forth. Knowing this, we stand in our own ordinariness and surmise that God might also actually appear to us and break us open to the life of service hiding within everyday details. What an amazing opportunity we have, to discover our own language of call and God's own language of response — and to take responsibility, that as the times we live through become less ordinary, we ourselves become less ordinary in response to the needs of the times.

My family tells a story that when I was a girl of five or six years, I set about scribbling furiously on a large sheet of paper my mother had put down on the floor.

Crayons scattered around me, tongue stuck out in concentration, I worked the colors onto the page. The texture of the linoleum came up through the paper, adding surprise designs to my drawing, which seemed to appear like magic. My mother wandered by and asked me, "What are you drawing?"

"A picture of God," I replied.

My mother knelt down to deliver her disappointing news as gently as possible. "Oh honey, you can't do that.... Nobody knows what God looks like."

I hear that I did not even lift my gaze from the enthrallment of my artwork as I informed her, "They will, as soon as I'm done with my drawing."

Connection to what theologian Joan Chitester calls "the One whose heart beats with ours" is part of our natural human capacity. And though children often have a natural and confident connection with the Divine, in the long journeys through religious training and enculturation, many people become adults no longer sure what they think about God, whether they know what "God" is or what "God" looks like.

In my own journey, the more I read, and the more I experience, the more mysterious the Divine becomes. I grew up a Protestant Christian with the Lord as my shepherd and little squares of white bread and grape juice served once a month in church. I marveled over the elaborate prayers of playmates who wore white veils to their first communion and prayed to Mother Mary and a host of what I called "the saints and saintesses." Down the road, if I stayed till Friday dusk at Howie Bernstein's house, his mother sang exotic prayers, lit candles, and sent me home with a piece of warm challah in my hand.

In my twenties, I grounded my spirit in Quaker Meeting and social activism, followed by eclectic reading in world religions, and adult confirmation as an Episcopalian. My religious training has been augmented by insights from indigenous spiritual traditions; studies in shamanism and Celtic spirituality; practices in yoga, chi gong, and vipassana meditation; and long walks in nature with my dog. All I know is there are a thousand faces of the Divine, and a thousand ways to pray. Every minute of life presents an essential choice: to avail ourselves of this relationship, or to close up in isolation.

We know there is power in spirit that can answer our prayers and change our lives, but we may not be sure what to pray for, or how ready we are to have our lives changed, thank you very much, God. We know there is power in spirit that can decode the mystery of life, but it's Tuesday, and we have a long list of things to do. We put off our willingness to entertain spiritual transformation day by day. Yet, no matter how ambivalent we are, no matter how liberal or conservative our religious and spiritual views, our longing for active relationship with *something greater than ourselves* cannot be forever denied. This longing may be the capacity that saves us in times like these. It is not a movement toward a specific religion, or away from religion: it is a movement to reclaim a personal relationship with the Divine.

Among humankind are millions and billions of good-hearted, good-natured, well-meaning people. I believe these people — including you and me — can redirect the course of history. We have already started. Millions of us are willing to reappraise social and personal values, and even change core beliefs, based on new and increasing information and insight about the world. Millions of us contribute to the common good through billions of small and yet significant acts of kindness and compassion. And millions of us are looking for some connection to spirit so real, so unmistakably authentic, that it will release our capacity to make an enormous shift in how we treat each other and the world.

Sometimes I think of the connection to spirit as being like a phone line. The connection is always open: it's our half of the relationship to stay available for incoming calls. Sometimes I turn the ringer off. Sometimes I ignore the ringing. Sometimes I pick up the phone with suspicion. Sometimes I hang up in anger. Sometimes I get impatient at the interruption. Sometimes I have no idea how to respond. The problem is not in the sending, but in the receiving. And unlike a lot of other calls, the one from spirit is the one we are hoping to receive.

One time, having tea with a friend, we were deep in conversation when the phone rang. I ignored it, thinking I was being polite. Jerry stopped his thought mid-sentence and asked, "Aren't you going to get the phone? Maybe God is calling you." I looked at him in amazement, reached for the receiver, and tentatively said, "Hello? . . . " I don't remember who was calling, but I have never forgotten Jerry's message to stay curious, to see if I can decode the Divine in everyday interactions. We have in ourselves some mysterious ability, in ordinary moments and moments of extreme, to speak with the voice of God — like the man who phoned from the World Trade Center with one last, brilliant message.

In the midst of all this searching, I wake in my house to the first light of day. I go out on the tiny balcony that bulges off the second floor office of my home and stand in the morning air. Usually I'm still wrapped in my bathrobe, sometimes leaning over the railing to watch the garden below, sometimes pressed back under the eaves to keep out of wind or rain. Usually I have a cup of tea in hand, and a corgi dog curled at my feet. Together we look at the day. I stand among tall trees that encircle my house and frame the view. I imagine putting down my own roots in the rocky clay soil. I watch creatures go by, the neighbor's cat, a suburbanized deer. A bird starts singing and I join it. I remember my own creatureliness, bow to my utter dependence on earth to sustain me and spirit to guide me. Then I say my daily prayer.

The heart of this prayer is a list: a string of seven directions that came into my mind over a period of several months. I think of them as an ecumenical mantra. Their language is universal. We can observe them inside any spiritual or religious tradition and follow them according to the dictates of personal conscience. They are short, memorable phrases that can be recited as prayer and remembered in moments of need.

I think of them as whispers of spiritual common-sense:

Maintain peace of mind.
Move at the pace of guidance.
Practice certainty of purpose.
Surrender to surprise.
Ask for what you need and offer what you can.
Love the folks in front of you.
Return to the world.

If every day the Divine is attempting to communicate its larger wisdom, then one of the most important things we can do is find a way to listen to spirit.

Reciting these seven whispers is a very simple practice.

It doesn't require physical training or stamina.

We don't have to travel to exotic and holy sites.

We don't even have to get out of bed.

This is the practice — recite and see what happens.

Call and see what responds.

Notice how help comes.

⚜ Maintain Peace of Mind

There is a really deep well inside me.
And in it dwells God.
Sometimes I am there too.
But more often stones and grit block the well,
and God is buried beneath.
Then He must be dug out again.

Etty Hillesum, *An Interrupted Life*

If the doors of perception were cleansed, said Blake,
everything would appear to man as it is   infinite.
But the doors of perception are hung with cobwebs of thought,
prejudice, cowardice, sloth. Eternity is with us, inviting our
contemplation perpetually, but we are too arrogant to still our
thought and let divine sensation have its way.

Evelyn Underhill, *Practical Mysticism*

Peace of mind is the cornerstone of spiritual life. It is the *tabula rasa*, the clean slate, upon which messages of spiritual guidance may be written. The only way I can receive these messages is to hold myself in a quiet, receptive state I call peace of mind. Here is the image that comes: With outstretched hands, I am holding a shallow bowl. The bowl is filled with clear water. The bottom of the bowl is lined with pebbles and shells that represent all the things that clutter my mind: extraneous thoughts, feelings, tasks, commitments — the stuff of life. I stare through the water, and see the busyness of my life slightly altered by the sheen of stillness. I am separate from my doing, waiting and calm. This peace of mind is where all spiritual direction starts, and to keep finding our way, we need to keep returning to this state of calm mind and open heart.

Unfortunately, our minds are not trained for stillness. Our thoughts are more often occupied by a highly opinionated, contentious committee of interesting and annoying characters. We may stand before the mirror and see one face looking back at us, but inside is the irrepressible child, the overbearing critic, the whiny victim, the encourager, the doubter, the judge, and so on. It takes years to sort through enough of these voices to have even a chance to serve as moderator of our inner committees, to stop feeling like a servant, constantly at beck and call to the lords and ladies of conflicting impulses.

In the decade of my thirties, I spent significant time and money in psychotherapy learning to assert my autonomy, to become my own self, and to master my fate. This did not bring me peace of mind, though it did install an internal set of Robert's Rules of Order. Henry Martyn Robert was an American army engineer who wrote these rules in 1876 to prevent overt violence in the raw terrain of pioneer society-making. Robert's Rules of Order were a profound success and have become a cornerstone of social conduct. They have had similar success within me, as I rarely draw blood while doing battle with my mind. No amount of therapeutic intervention, however, provided me with peace of mind.

Therapy is one of the popular paths of our time, but people have always done this mental sorting through various spiritual traditions, seeking to understand the mystical invitation the universe offers the human mind. In the opening quote, English mystic Evelyn Underhill, writing in 1915, quotes William Blake, who wrote in 1790. Peace of mind is a spiritual state waiting for us to find it. It has always been a possibility understood by monks and mystics, but in times like these the world needs you and me, ordinary people, to undertake this journey, to learn to step outside the ego self and find our spiritual self. To experience peace of mind, we need to expand beyond psychological clarity and learn how to comfortably experience a wider range of consciousness. This is not as difficult or mysterious as it may sound; we have been doing it spontaneously all our lives.

As a child of about six, I remember climbing a sycamore tree across the street from our house in Indianapolis. I scampered high enough in the branches to feel the tree moving in the wind, wrapped my sturdy legs around the smooth bark of the trunk, and hung on. The wind and tree held me and I became one with the sway. Enthralled. Enraptured. Ecstatic. We try to put this communion with the world into words, but during the actual experience, the mind is wiped clear of explanation and we exist in a pure state of relationship. We may call this wider range of consciousness daydreaming or lost moments, prayer or meditation. Our brains are wired for these beyond-word experiences. We just need help remembering how to let them into our awareness. Help remembering how to let them occur and surprise us in the midst of the everyday.

Decades ago when I was beginning to sort my psychological kitbag, I took a roll of masking tape and laid out sixteen-inch squares on the kitchen floor of my apartment. I labeled the squares: happy child, frightened child, angry child, punishing parent, loving parent, observer self, total confusion. As I worked with the stories and emotions rising up in me, I would stand in one square after another, hopscotching around in my self-parts. This experiment taught me to experience internal boundaries, and to shift from one state of mind to another.

My hopping about was often accompanied by long journal entries, through which I learned to identify who was being "me" at any given moment. And if I lost track of myself, I could stand on a stool and consider the options. Over time, I learned that shifting my sense of my "self" at any particular moment would also shift my emotional state, my thought processes, and my assumptions about the present moment. If I got stuck on a particular square, I could notice whether or not I was communicating clearly with myself and others, and decide which square was likely to be more effective. Eventually I spent more and more time in the observer self, negotiating among my psychological parts, and so established my moderator role with "the internal committee" or ego. I also noticed there was more to myself than represented in any one of these squares, and so began my spiritual odyssey.

If I were to do this exercise again today, the squares would be occupied by the cast of characters who emerged from psychological healing — integrated child, integrated self-parent, observer mind, and so forth — as well as characters who are surfacing during my spiritual journey. When I step outside the confines of personality, I find myself entering an expansive chamber of the mind where I cohabit with spirit. In this experience of cohabitation are sources of guidance that are not small self, but may be higher Self or soul: *she who listens, she who asks, she who prays, she who volunteers for service, she who challenges.*

One of my great teachers about all this is a woman named Etty Hillesum, whose diaries record her spiritual journey in the Netherlands as World War II began and the Germans invaded. Etty, a bright young Jewish woman moving about the intellectual café society of Amsterdam, began recording her insights and struggles as the world closed in around her. In 1941, she already understood what I was discovering on the kitchen floor. "[Y]ou can't think your way out of emotional difficulties," she wrote, "that takes something altogether different. You have to make yourself passive then, and just listen. Re-establish contact with a slice of eternity."

When we can be aware of the fullness of our self/Self, and live at least part of the time aware of this state of spiritual cohabitation, God is no longer far away in heaven. God is right here in the chambers of our hearts having tea, and reminding us, whisper by whisper, that we are not alone. When Brother Wayne Teasdale was researching his book *The Mystic Heart*, he found that when he asked people in the West, "Where is God?" they tended to point to heaven. When he asked people in the East the same question, they pointed to their chests. I suspect both are true: the Divine is above-below-behind-before, and the Divine is within. The purpose of any spiritual practice is to keep us engaged and in dialogue with the Divine, wherever we perceive it, and however we have learned to speak and listen.

At the beginning of the twentieth century, Evelyn Underhill wrote, "this state is not so much a rare and unimaginable operation, as something [we are] doing in a vague, imperfect fashion at every moment of conscious life, and doing with intensity and thoroughness in the more valid moments of that life." She calls this receptivity to dialogue letting "divine sensation have its way."

For me to let divine sensation have its way, I need a daily practice that fosters peace of mind. While I take responsibility for the peace I bring to the moment, I don't always feel very peaceful. When my mind is stirred up, and the water in my little bowl of tranquility is frothing with miniature whitecaps, I restore calm by practicing the most basic centering exercise there is: conscious breathing. I slow down and breathe in a way that rolls past the committee's busy voices and aerates the quiet corners of the mind. I take long, round breaths that expand into my belly. And often I follow the simple teaching of Vietnamese monk Thich Nhat Hanh: I take one breath to *let go*, one breath to *be here*, one breath to ask *now what?*

The thing about breathing is we can do it in public and nobody thinks we're weird. Breathing doesn't require accessories, special training, or equipment. Just breathing. We're doing it anyway; we might as well do it in a way that brings us closer to peace of mind.

I step out on the balcony of my house. I like to go outside, whatever the weather. The morning waits, or the afternoon, or the evening. I am standing among tree limbs with my yard and garden below. I take a few deep breaths. In our bodies, oxygen feeds the heart and brain first. To pause and breathe deeply literally sends more energy to the parts of our bodies we most need to access for peace of mind. Inhalation leads to inspiration.

One breath to *let go*.

Let go of the list making, the squabbling, the disorientation of too many selves, the confusion of priorities, the constrictions of the heart. Let go of my fears, the niggling of inadequacy, anger at this or that interaction, the rush that comes from taking things personally. Send in the oxygen, instead of the adrenaline.

One breath to *be here*.

Be here in the moment and notice what is: the sensual reality of wherever I am standing. Peace is all around me; my job is to bring my mind to peace. To *be here* is to step out of the center of the world, and to simply join it. What do I see, hear, taste, touch, smell — even through a plate glass window in a hotel lobby — how am I, here in the world?

One breath to ask *now what?*

Now what is trying to happen in my life? Now what

do I want this period of my life to mean? Now what might spirit say, if I say nothing more and just for a moment...listen.

I breathe. I whisper my request, "Please help me maintain peace of mind." The words echo in my skull. At its best, in this instance, my body feels like a hollow tube, flowing with gentle energy. My mind is receptive. I breathe, wait a few seconds, enjoy the stillness I am creating within myself.

Nobody taught me to do this, or else everything in my whole life has taught me to do this. I am simply practicing being *she who asks*, to see if *that which answers* has a message in this moment.

Beneath this phrase resides a whole paragraph of request: Please, God, keep me in the soul's council. Give me a split second to hear what You would say, to act as You would have me, to glimpse the larger purpose. Don't let me get swept up in the push-pull struggles of egotism — mine or anyone else's. Please think with me, and through me, so that I may maintain peace of mind in all that I do today.

Etty Hillesum, writing under far more strenuous conditions than my comfortable American life, spoke her covenant with God this way:

God, take me by Your hand. I shall follow You dutifully, and not resist too much. I shall evade none of the tempests life has in store for me, I shall try to face it all as best I can. . . . I shall never again assume, in my innocence, that any peace that comes my way will be eternal. I shall accept all the inevitable tumult and struggle. I delight in warmth and security, but I shall not rebel if I have to suffer cold, should You so decree. I shall follow wherever Your hand leads me and shall try not to be afraid. I shall try to spread some of my warmth, of my genuine love for others, wherever I go.

Etty Hillesum died in Auschwitz, November 30, 1943. She was twenty-nine years old. I read her diaries over and over, in awe of her insights as I send my little requests into the morning air, asking for accompaniment as I answer the phone, respond to email, interact with family, friends, colleagues, neighbors, and strangers.

How many decisions flow through our lives in the course of a day? Now, as it has always been, the constant little acts of yes and no, of welcome and refusal, shape who we are and determine where we're going. I want to make these choices within a spiritual context, and that is what I pray for with these words.

Some days I am not peaceful at all! My mind is seething with anxiety over how my life is going — whatever concern fills the moment: money, relationship, health, work, the latest bad news. So every day, here is my choice: to escalate the mantra of anxiety, or to take a few deep breaths and say firmly to myself: *this seems like as good a time as any to maintain peace of mind!*

And then I turn back to my desk and the imperfection of being myself. But at least I have taken a few moments to engage the mystery of the day. I have prayed first: before interacting with the rest of the family, before making breakfast, before getting to work. And such a prayer connects me to every other life, to all the ordinary people holding out our hands in faith that the great invisible Divine will reach back so that we may go into the day escorting each other.

The specifics of a morning ritual may be creatively designed to fit many different circumstances. Some of my friends do devotional reading, some meditate, some jog or take quiet early morning walks, some have coffee and heartfelt council in bed with their partner. I go out on the balcony, or if I'm not at home, find any little spot outside — the deck at my brother's house, a potted tree by the hotel entrance, a geranium blooming in a strange neighborhood. The commitment is to take a few minutes to bow down with the day and make myself available.

It's not so important what any of us do in the morning to invite peace of mind, it's only important that peace of mind is invited. That's the thing — to extend the invitation for divine sensation to present itself; to remember to prepare ourselves to walk the day in a spiritual manner. And then to listen, and to the best of our abilities do as we are told.

❧ Move at the Pace of Guidance

If a person feels a longing to be at one with the universe,
it is as if the universe feels the same longing
to be at one with the person.
If I sense a great aching in my heart to be in love with God,
it seems that God must in some mysterious way
share that aching for me.

Gerald May, *Will and Spirit*

In a world of speed and distraction, pace of guidance invites us to combine the practices of measured movement and listening. Speed is some guy running through the airport shouting into a cell phone. Pace is going around the block with a three-year-old and noticing everything the child is noticing.

When we move at pace, we have time to question and time to listen for answers before moving on. When we move at the pace of guidance, it occurs to us to wonder what plans the Divine might have for us, in the midst of the plans we have for ourselves.

Speed tends to cancel out guidance. When we move in speed, we are out of touch with spirit, and when we are out of touch with spirit, the ego steps into control. "After all," I hear that old familiar voice say in my mind, "somebody has to be driving!" And drive it does. Personal will runs rampant, like a headstrong horse.

I long ago discovered that the only way to stop a runaway horse is by first calming myself and then calming the animal. No amount of screaming helps. No amount of pleading. No amount of waiting for instructions from the roadside. The horse will run until it has run itself out, or I will find a way to slow the momentum and come back into relationship with what I am riding: becoming two beings moving with one gait.

I remember being thirteen years old, riding the Palomino mare I had just bought with three years of babysitting money and saved allowance. My father, having been raised in Montana, assumed that riding was in my genes. He gave me a few instructions and encouraged me to start walking Taffy around the yard and up and down the half-mile long cul-de-sac where we lived at the edge of suburbia. Taffy and I had been getting to know each other for two weeks when something spooked her that Saturday afternoon. I didn't even own a saddle yet, having spent all my money on the horse.

We were at the turnaround end of Oak View Lane when she took off and began flying down the gravel road, with me clinging to her back with all the strength I could muster in my still sore thighs. Past Larsen's house, past Grandprey's, past Rowbottom's, and Sundeen's. My father leaned on his shovel — he was still digging fence-post holes for the backyard corral — and beamed proudly as I hurtled by. I wanted to yell, "Don't smile! I'm not having fun! How do you stop this thing?"

Forty years later, I sometimes find myself wanting to shout these exact same words about my whole life.

Many times, the list of details I'm trying to manage is so long and complex that the end of my day simply consists of turning my back on whatever didn't get done. I leave my desk feeling I just can't cope anymore, not that I have reached a point of satisfaction. And then I wake at 3 A.M. and discover my mind is working while I sleep — the list is right there, organizing itself for the next day. I get up, go to the bathroom, and write notes to myself under the tiny glow of the nightlight, then slip back into bed and pray I can sleep again until dawn.

This is not life. Life is about being fully present, not allowing ourselves to become *doing machines*. If we want to hold our lives in any kind of spiritual context, we cannot be driven forward by our technology, demanding that our minds kick back nanosecond responses to delicate and complex issues. Machines do not have relationships with families and friends. Machines do not raise children. Machines do not have to fix supper, do the laundry, clean the house. Machines do not need exercise and time to play with the dog. Machines do not watch the sunset in utter amazement, even if that is the image flashing on their screensaver. We must hang onto our humanity; it is why we're in the world. We are a one-of-a-kind species, and we are at a crucial turning point in our evolution.

The pace of guidance, like peace of mind, begins internally — in me. Even though all my conditioning teaches me to accommodate speed, I am responsible for the *pace* I bring to the moment, just as I am responsible for the *peace* I bring to the moment.

This whisper combines two instructions: One, to rehumanize our speed of life, and two, to use this slower pace to actively listen for spiritual guidance. When we slow down, when we become receptive, we are able to hear a little voice that seems to arise within us. This voice is not the clattering monologue of our internal committee, but a voice that invites a dialogue only we can hear.

When we are engaged in spiritual dialogue, we are in a state of "call and response." Any form of prayer — from formal kneeling in the church pew, to a yelp of "oh sh*t!" as disaster strikes — is a call. Any signal — from a command we hear inside our minds, to a sense of an invisible touch on the shoulder, or a person who shows up and delivers a sentence that changes our lives — is a response.

The more broadly we can define call and response in our lives, the more we will see how the world within and around us is inviting our attention to guidance.

Over time, attending to guidance becomes a process of heightening our awareness of the ongoing flow of information and insight that is all around us, like the air through which we walk. Like the air, guidance is the medium in which we live and breathe. Spiritual guidance is with us, providing invisible, interactive support, right to the cellular level. One breath to let go . . . one breath to be here . . . one breath to ask, now what?

In my own life, I stumbled upon the direct connection to guidance at a time when I didn't know what to do next. In the midst of my frustration and confusion I made a commitment to sit in silence for at least fifteen minutes in the morning and again for fifteen minutes at the end of the afternoon. I went downstairs, arranged a few pillows, put a notepad and pen next to me in case a helpful insight came, and plunked down to breathe.

I didn't have much training in what I was doing, but now I recall a section from Joseph Campbell's *The Power of Myth* in which he talks about clearing a space in the day and making ready for insight. He says: "You must have a room or a certain hour of the day when you do not know what was in the morning paper, when you do not know who your friends are, you don't know what you owe anybody or what they owe you — but a place where you can simply experience and bring forth what you are, and what you might be.... At first you may find nothing's happening.... But if you have a sacred place and use it...something will happen."

Of course silence on the outside and silence on the inside are two different things. My mind was screaming with instructions, directions, anxieties. I decided to pose two questions to my soul:

What do you want me to do?

How do I need to change in order to do it?

Twice a day — almost every day — for three months, I sat in a little downstairs room fulfilling my commitment. The first month the only response to my questioning was "I want you to be quiet...." I learned to watch thought without attaching to it — to see thought as though it were a leaf twirling in the invisible wind. *Oh, I see that I expect X to happen. Oh, I see that I am telling myself an interesting story about this event or person. Oh, I see that I have forgotten to notice my breath.* And over and over again to simply return to watching breath.

This form of meditation comes from the Buddhist tradition of vipassana, or insight meditation. At this time in my life I had attended several silent meditation retreats led by Catholic nuns who were teaching vipassana to anyone interested. The use of conscious breathing, and other techniques to get beyond our obsession with thoughts, is a time-honored practice in many religious traditions. And so, in desperation over my inability to think my way through my current dilemma, I went to a little room in the middle of my life to seek spiritual guidance.

After the first month, my routine got a bit easier. So then I began to find excuses for not doing it. I was bored. What good was sitting there when I ought to be doing something relevant to solving my problem? However, most days of the week, I still made it down-stairs, fluffed the pillows, and asked my two questions:

What do you want me to do?

How do I need to change in order to do it?

As I worked with my impatience I noticed how my relationship with spirit sounded a lot like a child's relationship to a parent: "Please, God, gimme some guidance...and give it to me now!" I was forty years old at the time, and I realized the leap I was trying to make in my work life was also a leap I needed to make in my spiritual life.

If I wasn't going to be "God's little girl" anymore, what kind of relationship would I develop with the Divine? I began a series of dialogues written through ritual. I'd light a candle, center myself with a few breaths and words of prayer, and ask a leading question. The "Godalogues" went something like this:

Me: I'm depressed, angry, and scared. I believe these feelings are obsolete, but things seem so hard. Am I doing something wrong?

God: No. This transition is really hard, but hard is a judgmental word. Let's just say it is genuinely difficult because you are leaving behind most of your life training.

Me: I feel isolated and alone most of the time.

God: I'm here. Your loneliness is only a game your ego plays with you. Would you rather be more like ego or more like spirit?

Me: More spirit, less ego. I don't understand how come I'm on this cycle of up/down, win/lose emotionality when I'm doing what I feel directed to do.

God: You are doing the correct things. You are doing them in incorrect ways. Using old patterns, old thoughts, old fears and angers to motivate yourself.

Me: How do I replace old patterns?

God: Replace everything with joy. With confidence. With faith. With love. This difficult time in your life is a gift, because it is teaching you to keep seeking even when mundane reality invites you to feel victimized.

And so on and on the Godalogues went.

Where did this material come from? I don't know. I watched the dialogue emerge on the computer screen as I typed, and felt as though "I" were a third party, listening to two other parts of myself communicate. I'd type out a sentence, and the response would be instantly, fully, in my mind. Maybe this was conversation between my self and my soul. As I learned to trust how language would leap into my mind from a mysterious source, the voice of guidance became unmistakable.

This little voice has authority not because it speaks with power, but because it comes from power. Guidance addresses us philosophically, without embellishment. *(You are a spiritual being having a human experience.)* Or guidance speaks in brief instructions that do not beg for argument. *(Call your father, right now.)* Guidance encourages and warns us. *(Slow down, danger ahead.)* This voice in the mind is so persistent that it even speaks to those who don't believe it, and guides those who ridicule it. We distrust this voice, tell ourselves that we are making it up, and yet it is a phenomenon that has always been part of human experience.

At her heresy trial in 1431, the young mystic Joan of Arc was questioned by church authorities about the source of guidance she heard inside her head. "Are these not simply your imaginings?" the inquisitors asked her. She replied calmly, "How else would God speak to me, except through imagination?"

For myself there finally came a day when a complete and stunning response to my two questions rose in my imagination. The "now what?" got answered and I knew with certainty what I was supposed to do. I grabbed my notepad and wrote out directions as they were offered.

I had been stuck for months in my career as a teacher and writer, and was seeking help to find a new project. I had already written several books but was dissatisfied with the current direction in my work and didn't have a sense of how to move on.

What do you want me to do?

"Write this down," said the voice, "Life's Companion, Journal Writing as a Spiritual Quest. Write your way into the universe and draw on the wisdom behind the Godalogues. Do you think you are alone? Many people are questioning. Help gather the seekers. Walk the mystery together." In the next few minutes an entire curriculum, which later became a book outline, spilled onto my tablet pages.

How do I need to change in order to do it?

"See emotions as a form of weather, as changeable as the sky. When you have fear, put up your umbrella and keep walking. When you have joy, take off your sweater and enjoy the sun," the voice whispered. That was 1986.

Listening to the voice of guidance is not a one-time, okay-now-I-got-it, don't-have-to-practice-it kind of skill. It is, moment by moment, noticing whose voice I am listening to. Noticing which square I am standing in. Noticing whether or not I am paying attention.

One way I have trained myself to pay attention is to ask the next right question, one or two questions at a time, to see where the questioning itself might lead me. Right now I am asking a question that has to do with speed.

Coping with speed has become the heroic journey that consumes the lifetimes of the common man and woman. It is our greatest killer. Rushing puts us into adrenaline overload and drenches the body in epinephrine, a hormone stimulated by stress, anger, or fear. Epinephrine increases heart rate, blood pressure, cardiac output, and carbohydrate metabolism. While epinephrine has legitimate uses in the body, a constant internal stimulation of the fight-or-flight response does not help us move at the pace of guidance.

We know what the *speed* of life looks like. We don't, however, have much information about the pace of guidance. So I am asking: *How do I move at the pace of guidance, no matter what speed the world asks me to move?* I don't have the answer, but just as I learned to carry my questions down to my little room, I'm carrying this question with me into each day. The question interrupts my automatic behavior. It helps me watch my choices, stay out of stress, and maintain peace of mind as I walk through the day.

All those years ago, when I was clinging to my

runaway horse, the end of Oak View Lane intersected with the highway coming out of downtown. As the horse and I raced toward it, I could hear traffic going by and I prayed Taffy would have enough sense not to run broadside into a car. I prayed I would have enough sense to slow her down. I leaned down on her neck, trying to keep my buttocks on her bouncing back. I could feel my thighs trembling with strain against her ribs. "Whoa, girl...whoa, Taffy, calm down. Calm down. We can do this. Whoa now." I pulled back on the reins, feeding the leather through my hands. Everything was sweaty — the horse, myself, the leather sliding in my palms. The highway was just ahead. As we hit the shoulder I pressed the rein firmly against her neck and turned her onto the pavement's edge as she slowed to a bouncing trot. Her feet hit asphalt — and the whole pace changed so suddenly I nearly fell.

Taffy began prancing, her delicate legs pulled up high against her chest, head high. Our manes picked up the breeze. I remembered now: before the boy who sold her to me, this Arabian mare had belonged to a Shriner who rode her in local parades. Taffy had switched from full gallop to parade dressage. Cars slowed down around us. People waved. I cautiously turned my magic steed back up the road home. We walked all the way. Two beings moving in one gait.

As so many girls who fanaticize about horses must learn, a horse is not just a big dog but a powerful animal I would never match and never control. It was very clear to me that afternoon that I did not stop that horse. It was not a matter of me exerting strength or willpower over Taffy. Riding her was an agreement between us: a willingness on her part to let me on her back, and a readiness on my part to set our course and manage the pace. It was clear to me that riding my horse would never go exactly as I imagined. She and I would always be in a conversation of words and signals, suggesting and counter-suggesting the best route for the journey — step by step, ride by ride. In exchange for the wind in her face, and care in the paddock, she would carry me into moments of grace and train me for bravery.

Looking back, it occurs to me to wonder if perhaps the momentum of life is a living being. *What if the speed and distraction that is driving us out of our minds is an invitation to develop the capacity to leap into timelessness?*

Whizzing about in our machinery, we think of speed

in a mechanistic way. Our most revered inventions are those things that go the fastest: sports cars, computers, jets, and rockets. We celebrate and lament life in the fast lane. Life on the treadmill. Networking. Interfacing.

Instead, what if we see this day as a living, breathing being of energy and power, with which we can develop a capacity to transcend the rush of details? Just when we think it's domesticated, this living momentum will show us its wild side. Just when we are shouting for help and pulling back on the reins, we will come into stride with whatever we are riding. When we are both tired, we can walk. We can sit by the river sipping cool, clear water. We can trust that in stopping, the wisdom for proceeding will find us.

It's still our job every morning to saddle up and ride. It's our job to get back on when we fall off. It's our job to groom and tend and feed the momentum so that when we need to let it loose, we have the skills to ride with the wind. It's our job to let the Divine blow in our faces and guide us home.

❧ Practice Certainty of Purpose

There is no one but us.
There is no one to send,
nor a clean hand nor a pure heart
on the face of the earth, nor in the earth, but only us,
a generation comforting ourselves with the notion
that we have come at an awkward time,
that our innocent fathers are all dead   as if innocence had ever been
*   and our children busy and troubled,*
and we ourselves unfit, not yet ready,
having each of us chosen wrongly,
made a false start, failed,
yielded to impulse and the tangled comfort of pleasures,
and grown exhausted, unable to seek the thread, weak, and involved.
But there is no one but us.
There never has been.

Annie Dillard, *Holy the Firm*

Practicing certainty of purpose is a commitment to figure out *why we are here and what we are going to do about it*. When we practice certainty of purpose, we balance our personal will to fulfill certain needs and desires with an awareness that our individual lives affect the needs and desires of the larger community.

Following certainty of purpose is like listening for my particular melody line to hum in the midst of a complex piece of music. Everybody is listening, and humming. Sometimes it's a confusing cacophony, and sometimes the harmony is marvelous. But there is no one but us, there never has been.

I think of it this way: if all humanity is one body, I am one single cell, perhaps residing on a freckle near the left elbow of this universal whole. It doesn't seem like one cell has that much influence over the whole body, but each contributes to harmony or disharmony. If one little cell is malignant, cancer can spread until the whole body is threatened. This is a lesson very much with us in the world's body right now. If one little cell is doing the very best job it can at being a freckle, then well-being can also spread until the whole body is healthy. This is a lesson we are trying to learn. I may never understand, or even want to try to understand, why I'm the little cell that I am. I may never be able to see how my actions affect the larger whole. This is where faith comes in.

There is a legend in the Hasidic tradition that says when a baby is conceived an angel accompanies the soul into the womb and lives with the fetus for the nine months of gestation. Here, in the blood-thumping shelter of the mother, angel and soul speak of the life to come and decide together on the purpose of this incarnation: *What is this soul coming to contribute? Who will help support this purpose? What challenges will be faced? Where comes love? How will death find this one and bring him or her home?*

Of course, such a story-loving tradition would imagine that even before birth, story is made of life. Of course such a dialogue-based religion would imagine a Hasidic angel, black curls and white wings, in discourse with the soul inside the tiny growing body. There is, of course, a catch to all this thoughtful planning.

Just as the birth pangs begin, when the soul must fully enter the baby-self and the angel return to heaven, the angel reaches out and presses its finger against the baby's lip. We still have this mark, an indentation that runs sweetly from upper lip to nose. The philtrum is the angel's last gift. "Hush," it whispers to the stirring child, "now you must forget." And all the while the womb bears down around us, pushing us out into the waiting world. Here we come, imbued with purpose and arriving in amnesia. Newborn.

But we are not total amnesiacs. Small children delight and sometimes shock us with their abilities to both remember and predict things about their lives, their families, their futures. Just before her fourth birthday, my niece Erin inquired sweetly, "Auntie Christina, how did we meet?"

"I went to the hospital the day after you were born," I told her. "They rolled you out in your little pink bassinet and I stood there and stared at you — all tiny and new, asking, now who is this who's come into my life."

"Not then," she firmly responded. "Don't you remember? When did we really meet?"

British poet William Wordsworth wrote a classic statement of his belief in innate certainty of purpose.

Our birth is but a sleep and a forgetting:
The soul that rises with us, our life's star,
Hath elsewhere had its setting,
And cometh from afar:
Not in entire forgetfulness,
And not in utter nakedness,
But trailing clouds of glory do we come
From God who is our home.

Most of us live in this paradox: we are trailing glimpses of insight, knowing why we are here, and not knowing. We both remember, and forget. We are imbued with wonder, and sometimes consumed with loss. From childhood on, we seek our purpose in a thousand ways.

Once I was a girl setting the table on a winter's evening. There is the light of the household gathering for supper, my mother is in the kitchen, younger children are playing boisterously nearby. The family is waiting for the father whose arrival home from a day's work will signal the time to eat. My job is to set out knives, forks, spoons, plates, and napkins. I look up and realize it has grown dark outside. I slip out the side door, through the screen porch, and into the chilled night air.

Arms wrapped around my torso, hugging myself against the onset of shivers, I recite: *Star light, star bright, first star that comes to light, I wish I may I wish I might have the wish I wish tonight.* I search the dusk for that first pinprick of faraway fire to emerge through the bare oak branches of the neighbors' trees and pray, *Please, God, let me have my full life.* I wait a few seconds in the silence, breathing a small cloud in front of my face, then turn back and rejoin the household.

Certainty of purpose starts by believing we have one. From the front porch of my childhood home, the longing for purpose led me to Europe in my twenties in search of spiritual adventure. Later in life it led me from Minnesota to Washington, to live on an island at the edge of the continent. This longing guides me in and out of relationships, sometimes with great confusion, sometimes with astounding clarity. It opens and closes me to various opportunities and adventures. It attunes me to the voice of guidance that rises within me.

One summer night in Paris, a wise young man whispered in my ear, "Inside each of us, the tree of our own life is growing. If this tree is too small for us, we shrink and wither around it and turn into a shrub. If this tree is too big, it becomes a giant oak that tears us apart. We grow in constant tension, so that we and our lives remain the right size for each other." This is a story I have remembered all the years since and referred to many times. I love this story because it creates a view of life that challenges the ways we diminish or falsely enlarge ourselves and expands the possibilities of who we think we are. It sets me wondering what size life I am willing to grow.

In my writing classes I often suggest that people write a story about themselves in the third person, so they can see their life purpose emerge first at a mythic level. It's a very simple exercise; we each complete the phrase:

Once there was a (man or woman) who . . .

Once there was a man who longed to leave the farm. The youngest son, he saw two brothers take up the plow and plant the corn. 'There is no room for me, here,' he thought. And so he began to look at the far horizon to see what would call him into the big, wide, world. . . .

Once there was a woman who did what she was told. She married a decent man and raised three good children. At age fifty she sat down on the porch amid the clutter of her youngest daughter's graduation party and wondered what she would do with the rest of *her* life. . . .

Almost automatically, these little stories reveal where we come from, who we think we are, and where we think we're headed. Sometimes they surprise us, revealing things we hadn't been aware of or articulating choices the mind has already made on our behalf. They have disarming power to speak what the soul knows about our lives, to reveal the angel's code.

Once I know my story on the metaphoric level — how I am the woman who grew out of the girl who stood on the family porch and prayed beneath the stars — I can shape a statement of purpose that informs the workaday levels of my life as well. This is not a "to do" list, but rather a "to be" list. I begin to write this statement with the phrase:

Right now in my life . . .

Right now in my life, I am committed to this book and supporting its work in the world. I am committed to the practice of circle and the work of our teaching. I see my partnership as soul-work that is as important as anything else we do. I choose to submit all my choices to spiritual purpose and make decisions every day by asking my soul for instruction.

There isn't a lot of security in being a self-employed visionary, and sometimes I fall into grave doubt. I have endured several intense periods of spiritual anguish. For me, certainty of purpose has often reemerged from those dark hours, when I am on my knees, gripping the balcony rails, pleading — "What do You want me to do, God?!" "Why am I here?" "Why did this happen?" "What am I supposed to learn?" And finally, finally, through some act of grace, I find my way back to a calm mind and open heart. Then I am able to lay out my skills and talents and reenter my dialogue with purpose. I can sit down again, teacup in hand and journal on my lap, take three breaths, and stop cursing my fate. I can lean back against the solid walls of my house, and look out at the world around me, and offer out to God, "Okay, this is what I've got.... What would serve thy purpose?"

The purpose of life is not to maintain personal comfort; it's to grow the soul. The willingness and struggle that carries people through the years must be grounded in our covenants with the angel. How else can we explain our determination? How else can we explain the varieties of human experience? The disparity of apparent ease and struggle?

I see people endure what to me would be unendurable, and use it to thrive because it is within their covenant. And I have seen people break under a load that looks lighter than my own.

Even in the most mainstream and comfortable lives, tension surfaces when the job is done, when the children are raised, when the busyness subsides and we are available to ask ourselves: *What is the new mystery that is calling me?*

I pray you will be able to answer this question. Please pray that I will be able to answer this question as well. We need each other to fulfill our destinies. The health, even the survival, of the human body is at stake. We know this, even if it's still Tuesday, when we are putting the voice of God on hold and tending to other, more important details. Tension is always present between the demands of being a "good freckle" on the left elbow of the whole, and looking up to see how our actions and lives contribute to the complex purpose humankind seems to be pursuing.

Among many of my friends we often speak of "doing the work." We are dedicated to doing this work. What "the work" is takes different forms, but we sense a common spiritual purpose connecting our efforts. One friend is a consultant, another a clergy, a teacher, a writer, a community organizer, a gardener, a drummer, a guide. When one of us falters, the others remind him or her: "You have a purpose. Do your work. Rest here. Find peace of mind. Ask for guidance. Fill yourself with certainty. Then move on. We're with you."

"The work" does not need to be grand, only fitting. It is guided by asking ourselves over and over: *What is the next right thing?* Maybe it's to rest after an arduous project or period of parenting. Maybe it's to reclaim creativity. Maybe it is to say "yes" or "no" to an opportunity. Maybe it's a new relationship, or reviving an old one. We have watched each other so many times come alive to the next right thing. Our hearts jump with excitement and we're off and moving at the pace of guidance.

One hot summer day, over a decade ago, I was driving alone on a backcountry road, wind roaring through open windows, hair wild and lashing around my face. I was on my way to a new teaching experience. Aware that it would take my life in a whole new direction, a sense of sudden alignment rose up in me. I recognized this moment, as though at some level I already understood the implications. I spent the next hour shouting insights into the wind. My words felt snatched from my mouth into the white noise. It was as if my angel was sitting in the passenger seat and we were engaged in exuberant conversation.

I know this experience isn't unique to me. It has been sung and written and told in a million stories. We long to know who we are. We long to know why we have come. We long for the fullness of our personal lives.

In her poem "Tonight Everyone in the World is Dreaming the Same Dream," poet Susan Litwak says it this way:

Each person lies in their bed, restless,
calling an unknown name.
An angel comes to each and every one
and says: "Choose one hand," its own hands
shimmering behind its back.
"In the right is life, in the left
death, called emptiness." At that moment
sobs are heard all over the earth,
and in the heavenly spheres
a rain of tears.

In the dream I am weeping,
For the angel has no hands,

only wings; and each person gazes
at their own palms, purified and glowing.
One hand holds a spark, the other
a dry coal. Each person
spreads their wings.
The earth is created, and moves us
on our journey
toward remembering.

I do not consciously remember anything I said in my afternoon conversation shouting at the wind blowing through my car, but I know I held the spark and am still moving on the journey declared in that epiphany. And I know there have been more surprises along the way than I could have ever imagined.

✤ Surrender to Surprise

My boat strikes something deep.
At first sounds of silence, waves.
Nothing has happened;
Or perhaps everything has happened
And I am sitting in my new life.

Rumi

Surprise is a chance to open something new. We can hardly resist shaking the unopened box, guessing at the contents, peeking under just a tiny corner of the wrapping. Life's surprises are sometimes delightful, sometimes painful. Life's surprises introduce unexpected elements and experiences we might not have the courage to choose. But eventually curiosity gets the best of us so that even an initially painful or bewildering surprise becomes a gift we are willing to open. Surprise encourages us to relate to experience with a sense of wonder. Surprise challenges us to be startled awake, and sometimes shocked to our core.

When we set intention and claim purpose, we often step forward with great certainty. But a gap always opens between what we think will happen, and what actually does happen. This gap is surprise. We may be maintaining peace of mind, moving at the pace óf guidance, and practicing certainty of purpose, but that does not mean we know how we're going to reach a goal, or who and what is coming along to help and hinder us in the journey.

When I was preparing to return to my college for the twenty-fifth reunion of my class, I pulled out several photos of graduation day, 1968. There I was, smiling confidently between my parents and laughing with friends, but one photo caught me standing in line to enter the auditorium, staring off into the unknown future. This was the image that intrigued me. In my journal, I wrote out a fantasy encounter between myself in 1993, and myself then. The forty-seven-year-old approached the twenty-two-year-old.

"Hello, Chrissie," *I at 47* wrote. "I just wanted to say that things are going to be okay, but won't turn out as you expect." *She at 22* looked at me blankly. My pen hurried on, "I mean you're not going to marry Tim. And your brother's about to be drafted to Vietnam, but he won't be killed. You'll get a job in San Francisco, just like you want, but you'll be living in Europe before you're twenty-five. You are going to have an unusual life, outside traditional marriage, outside traditional work. Even though you turned down graduate school, you're going to end up teaching, and writing books. Isn't that amazing! So, I wonder, do you have any questions?"

The *22 self* scrutinized this woman who was her mother's age. "I have just one question," she ventured. "Who the hell are you?" Who I am is the result of mixing certainty of purpose with surrender to surprise.

We engage this whisper on many levels. Surprise is the practice of accepting the unexpected interruption, and the practice of leaving enough space in the day for something to happen that isn't on the list. Surrendering to surprise is the practice of balancing structure and openness.

Nowadays, I get up, do my morning rituals, and show up at my desk. I sit with what's left there from yesterday, open my calendar, turn on the computer and look for email, write out a list of the day's "TO DOs." I usually separate these into categories: immediate work (write book, make business calls, answer all flagged emails), long-range work (follow-up with last month's group, send flyers, check in with office assistant), personal/family commitments (mail birthday card, make supper, call mother), spiritual/self-care (take long dog walk, eat wisely). Some people are far more organized than this. They work out hourly schedules on electronic organizers, bill by the minute, live with day-planners that run from 6 A.M. to midnight. Whatever we think we're doing in a day: there is still *surprise*....

It would hardly seem we need reminding about something so obvious as the fact that things are not going to go exactly as we plan. But when we have stopped expecting surprise, when we are moving along at great speed in a fantasy of control, even a traffic delay can be interpreted as a personal affront rather than a neutral event. A little more willingness to surrender to surprise might go a long way toward reducing the rage and anxiety that seem to be escalating in society.

Becoming aware of how surprise supports us is a spiritual skill. To live life consciously, we need to prepare for wonderful and horrible things to happen to us that we don't expect. Every day we need to notice when and how spirit is trying to get through our little fantasies of self-determination with some other message. Chart the day and look for the unexpected. Chart life with a spirit of openness.

I had an aunt who used to respond to any family crisis with the assurance, "When God shuts a door, He opens a window." She was reminding us to look differently at surprise. Right now in some churches you'll hear the refrain: "If God is good, then God is good all the time." This invites us to trust spirit as it works in our lives, even when surprise is not to our liking.

Surrendering to surprise allows us to practice the resilience we need to respond to whatever life offers. As we practice surrendering to smaller surprises, we build up the resilience required when larger surprises come along. A person who can miss all the green lights on the way to work and find a way to see it as a blessing is far better able to handle a layoff or missed promotion and figure out the blessing in that event as well.

There are three responses to surprise that help us practice spiritual surrender:

1. Notice what is really happening.
2. Work with what is really happening.
3. Accept what is really happening.

Several years ago, as I returned home on a bright spring afternoon from a week-long business trip, my little dog Willow leapt happily in and out of my lap in greeting, while I sat on the front steps reveling in her exuberance. We were having a wonderful time. (*Notice* what is really happening.) What I didn't know was that a few minutes earlier she had wandered into the neighbor's yard where they had just put out highly lethal slug bait. I got busy for a while, checking the mail and phone messages; then I called Willow and we headed for a trip around the block. After a few steps, her hindquarters did an unusual spasm. I could hardly believe my eyes. (*Notice* what is really happening.) We walked a little farther. She spasmed again, as though her hind legs were dancing without her permission. She turned around and looked at herself, then at me, in puzzlement. I had seen this once before, poison working on the central nervous system. (*Notice* what is really happening.) I grabbed her up in my arms and jogged back to the house.

"Call the vet," I shouted to my partner. "Willow's eaten poison." (*Work* with what is really happening.) We got in the car, and I drove to town. The whole way, Willow lay on the floor of the front seat, staring at me while I crooned to her confidently, "Don't worry, you'll be all right. You just have to throw up. The doctor will know what to do." (*Work* with what is really happening.)

The veterinarian tried everything and, when her heart stopped, performed CPR and brought out tiny electric paddles to get it going again. (*Work* with what is really happening.) I knelt in the grass by the clinic door and prayed furiously. Just before 6 P.M., they brought out her body and laid it in my arms. I hadn't been home two hours. Surprise.

We spent that night on my balcony. Willow wrapped in a blanket, stiff body curled in her dog bed, me in my robe with a pillow and a candle keeping vigil. All night I watched over her irrevocable stillness. Such a little act of carelessness. Such a little death. Such big consequences. Surrender.

Willow's death was not my first difficult surprise, of course, but additional struggles came with it. (*Accept* what is really happening.) First, we had to bury this loyal companion, digging a hole under her favorite tree, crying with the morning rain. Then I had to forgive my neighbors, not only for the death of one Welsh corgi, but also for putting poison around their flower beds next to my organic yard, for dealing differently in how they treat the earth. (*Accept* what is really happening.) Then I had to look at my own gardening practices, for the slugs crawled into our flowers and vegetables, too. Every night it was my practice to walk around the gardens with a flashlight and a squirt-bottle of ammonia diluted in water. Any slug caught in the act of garden trespass got sprayed, dissolving into writhing slime under my flashlight beam. How could I mourn death and deal out death at the same time? How could I commit myself to loving the earth and all its creatures and keep finding exceptions for those creatures who got in my way? (*Accept* what is really happening.) I stopped squirting slugs.

There are no guarantees in life. Good things happen to bad people and bad things happen to good people. And most of the time, it's not even personal, not based on merit or deficiency: we are just the next ones in line for the lesson. Being spiritual doesn't save us from anything. But being spiritual allows us to hold whatever happens in a spiritual way. When things happen, our underlying faith or doubt is brought to the surface. Most of us don't have trouble accepting what we think will be a good surprise. It's when the phone rings in the middle of the night, when the attorney's registered letter arrives, when the police officer gets out of the car and walks up our driveway, when the supervisor comes into our office and closes the door that the stomach turns over with a lurch and we recognize a different kind of surprise is upon us.

Here's the thing about gut-wrenching, heart-shaking, mind-changing surprise: it is a donation to our own growth. If we work it well, from this growth we can donate insight and action back into the well-being of the larger community. A mother struggling to make peace with the death of her child may become an advocate who changes conditions for other children and parents. A family who inherits some wealth may contribute to the land conservancy in their area. The letter to the editor I wrote after Willow's death, which encouraged people to communicate with their neighbors and to protect the lives of animals and children, was circulated in a five-state area over the Associated Press wire. Donation.

"Surrender" is not a word that rolls easily off the tongue in our privileged, dominant culture. We are programmed to consider ourselves conquerors, not surrenderers! "Believe it and achieve it!" shout the gurus of personal mastery. There is a different quality to us, however, once we have surrendered a few times to awful and awesome surprise.

Surrender is not easy work. The ego's drive for self-preservation and comfort do not allow us to sign up for life's hardest lessons voluntarily. Who would step forward if asked to volunteer for ill health? Bereavement? Disaster? Ruin and exposure? Imprisonment? Alienation? And yet we do handle these situations, or know those who are handling them.

In the closing paragraph of her book describing the autism of her daughter, Clara Claiborne Park writes:

> This experience we did not choose, which we would have given anything to avoid, has made us different, has made us better. Through it we have learned the lesson that no one studies willingly, the hard, slow lesson of Sophocles and Shakespeare — that one grows by suffering....I write now what fifteen years past I would still not have thought possible to write: that if today I were given the choice to accept the experience, with everything that it entails, or to refuse the bitter largesse, I would have to stretch out my hands because out of it has come, for all of us, an unimagined life. And I will not change the last word of the story. It is still love.

During one period of difficult surprise, I found myself again writing Godalogues in my journal. "Oh great Mystery," I wrote, "I ask that I might learn from this disaster and survive this learning. I ask for the chance to heal. For the chance to continue being of service with my life. Please help me understand."

And the faithful inner voice responded on the page:

I provide these trials because you have said "yes" to me. You have said you will stand at the gate with your sisters and brothers and come through together. To do this you must be able to withstand the terror and chaos that goes on in what you call the world. You can only serve the Light to the extent that you can stand the Dark.

So here is my challenge to your soul: to know the Dark, and not fight against it. To use this time to discover your strength, to see that wherever I put you, you are held in love. If you do not know this down to your very cells, how will you hold the door open for others? Of what service can you be to other people's fears? To their confusion?

You must be sure that spiritual transformation is possible. You must be sure that spiritual transformation is precisely the opportunity of the times, so that nothing can shake you, nothing can drive you away from this faith. The purpose of this occurrence in your life is to turn you inward, to see that you cleanse yourself of ambiguity, mistrust, denial, dishonesty in all its subtle forms, to give up all avoidance of disaster. I invite you to be fully *here*, to be spiritually dependable, to be fully obedient.

Spiritual dependability is not a one-time event, but choosing and choosing and choosing, in all the little and big surprises, to accept what is really happening and spin life's straw into gold.

There, I've said what I know to say about this. I get ready to save the file and move on. The word processor on my computer prompts me with a question both practical and profound: "DO YOU WANT TO SAVE THE CHANGES YOU MADE TO SURRENDER?" appears in a little box at the top of my screen.

"Yes," I say, and again, again, again. Yes. Surprise me. And here come two little corgi dogs to dance under my desk and between my legs. One is my partner's four-legged, named Gwen. The other is my new friend, Glory Be.

❧ Ask for What You Need
   and Offer What You Can

We clasp the hands of those who go before us,
and the hands of those who come after us;
we enter the little circle of each other s arms,
and the larger circle of lovers
whose hands are joined in a dance,
and the larger circle of all creatures,
passing in and out of life,
who move also in a dance,
to a music so subtle and vast
that no one hears it except in fragments.

Wendell Berry, Healing

A s a spiritual practice, when we ask for what we
need and offer each other what we can, we enter
a dance of unavoidable reciprocity. We are doing a
two-step exchange of needs and offerings, and the
whole village is dancing. If we pay attention, we discover we cannot give without receiving; we cannot

receive without giving. When a friend asks, "Can I give you a hug?" I wonder how she will give it to me without being in it with me? Or if someone says, "I need a hug," does he notice that his request requires my willingness to offer my arms?

Asking / offering / giving / receiving is one circular motion. If we don't ask for what we need, if we don't offer what we can, we block the dance. Imagine a person in the middle of the dance floor suddenly not moving while all around him continue on. People would start bumping into each other, losing the beat, losing their sense of direction, tripping over each other's toes. The dance is dependent on the dancers. Reciprocity is dependent on unceasing exchange.

As we ask for what we need and offer what we can we become spiritual traders of life's energy, time, abundance, and interrelatedness. Through this practice, we are reminded that *everything* lives in reciprocal relationship with everything else, whether or not we immediately perceive this relationship, whether or not we choose to be aware of it. Even though we often have an ambivalent relationship with reciprocity, not wanting to think about the times when we are the ones stopping the dance, we are inspired by it, over and over.

Though it was several decades ago, I remember an autumn dusk driving out of the city in rush hour when I noticed a young boy sitting on his bicycle in the grass median between lanes of busy traffic. The pack of cars on the boulevard was crawling along bumper to bumper, giving me time to watch him as I made my way up the block. A poor boy in a poor neighborhood of subsidized housing units. Boy of brown skin, watching white-faced drivers head home to houses he'd probably only seen on television. His demeanor began to change as he waited for a break in the lines of cars. Now he slumped across his handlebars, head down, resigned.

I knew nothing of his story, but I watched him through the eyes of commonality, because I do know what it is like to stand at the side, to hope for recognition, for entrance, for safe passage, for help. I turn on my flasher lights and roll to a halt, stopping my lane of traffic. I bleep my horn and signal the man next to me. We grin at each other and he, too, stops his lane of traffic. The boy raises his head. Before him the Red Sea is parting and he cannot believe his eyes. He looks through my windshield and straight into my heart. Our faces light up for each other, and with the greatest grin he jumps his rusty banana seat off the curb and wheelies around in the space created for him. And in his acceptance of this gesture, he creates for me a chance to celebrate exuberance. Confident now, he takes his time. Crossing the road like a magic dancer, he struts his stuff before us all, jumps the far curb, and rides off down a side street, head high and whooping. I know nothing of his story, but I remember this moment, and trust that he does, too.

Trading is practice in mindfulness. It slows us down so we may notice the opportunity present in the moment. Through acts of spiritual trading we learn to see that everything is an exchange. Today I will ask for what I need, first by becoming aware of what that is. Today I will offer what I can by holding all the choices I make within an understanding of reciprocity. The trajectory I set into the day is not a straight line; it's a dance of intersections and connections between myself and other people and the opportunities we create as we cross each other's paths.

I have a saying by Annie Dillard posted over my desk that reads: "How we spend our days is how we spend our lives." I have about sixteen hours of waking energy in a day. *How do I want to spend them? What will guide my choices?* My partner and some friends are going bicycling, but I need several hours of peace and quiet to write. I trade one experience for another. There is both loss and gain. I still need exercise and a sense that I have taken advantage of sun and fresh air, so I make time to walk the dogs. I trade their canine patience for the promise of a romp. I need help finding some references, so I call the library and the local bookstore. I need to know that my beloved and I are of like mind about a problem, so we talk over breakfast and trade solitude for togetherness.

Today I will offer what I can by being open to surprise and interruption as part of the flow of my intentions. An older neighbor calls to ask if I will bring her mail from the box to her doorstep. Of course I will, though I also know it means fifteen minutes of chatting. I trade a little efficiency for the aid I can provide a neighbor. Someday I will be old and in need of a younger person's kindness. A friend emails the request for a prayer chain for his son. I stop and light a candle on my windowsill, hold the thought of his need for a moment. Someday I will be in need of the prayers of friends and strangers. A client calls and asks for twenty minutes of consultation. As we enter our conversation, I trust that what she asks me to give will also serve my needs. A friend invites us for supper. I say no, not tonight, but I make a cup of tea and spend twenty minutes on the phone catching up and setting a date for the future. I trade the evening for the moment, because I want to honor our relationship even in my busyness. A solicitor calls and I say no, but I trade one minute of politeness to a stranger who may be working hard to pay her bills. Every yes and every no is held within the flow of trade and reciprocity.

Sometimes reciprocity is immediate and obvious, sometimes we may not see it for years, or may never see it, only trust the contribution has been made and received and passed along. And I am not doing this alone. Everyone is trading with everyone else. But not everyone is thinking about trade as a spiritual practice.

I recently chose to help a teenager through her first year of community college by lending her my car several days a week for the commute. I willingly added her to my insurance, kept up repairs, and worked my own needs for the car around her schedule. I entered this agreement to signal my long-term support for her and to provide an opportunity for the two of us to practice negotiating with each other. It was a very difficult offering because she didn't see much need to offer something back. We were not very successful in our negotiation practice, and she often used the car with an attitude of entitlement that left me feeling my kindness was abused. Many times I considered withdrawing my offer, wondering how to best help her see reciprocity as a necessary skill for entering adulthood.

It was a complex choice, and I let her continue using the car. I decided I had the stamina to make this offering and hold the tension of the trade without demanding that her understanding match mine. I will be curious to see if the gift of this support dawns on her over time. I will keep working with our relationship to instill a sense of spiritual trade. And I will keep track of my limits, for I am responsible to myself to see that I am indeed asking for what I need and only offering what I can.

Only spiritual trading creates flow. As long as the energy is flowing and cyclical, there is enough to go around. If any one of us stops asking or stops offering, the flow is disrupted and the balance destroyed. We all know people who give and give and give and forget to receive until they collapse into exhaustion, depression, or illness. We all know people who take and take and take and forget to offer until they find themselves alone at the zenith of their careers, divorced from their families and friends. If we become depleted, we have no energy left to respond and no energy left to ask. If we keep demanding without reciprocating, people will respond with resentment or hoard their energy and we will not get what we really need. Perhaps the purpose of this learning cycle, playing out over and over again in our lives, is to help us see the world differently.

Our Western cultural consciousness is saturated with competitive messages and assumptions that do battle with our spiritual yearnings. We talk about money and power and time as commodities, but we hardly know how to talk about energy exchange, shared power, or spiritual trade. There is an attitude out there (and in us) that if people are too dumb to take care of themselves, well, it's their own fault if they get taken advantage of. There is an attitude out there (and in us) that if we want something, and no one is holding onto it at the moment, well, it must be ours for the taking: land, oil, diamonds, market share, food, water, time, energy, attention.

All this confusion creates an enormous imbalance that extends all the way from our personal emotions and thought processes to the global economy. Along comes this little phrase that invites us to ask for what we need and offer what we can, and we discover it has a taproot that penetrates the subsoil of how we live in the world. This can make us very uncomfortable as our unconscious privilege comes to light, but if a growing number of us start living our lives as spiritual traders instead of as consumers or competitors, something *will* change in the world.

This is the whisper that calls us in the opulent West to accountability. Clattering about in our lives of too many things and too much to do, how do we learn to live simply, so that others may simply live? Really, what do we need? What do we offer? The rising interest in *feng shui*, in making sacred space out of our homes and offices, and in recycling all point to our awakening awareness of the need to simplify our lifestyles and make careful, conscious choices.

In the coming years, I believe that we in the West will be challenged as never before to look at the question of what we really need and what we have the obligation to offer in order to re-establish balance in the global human family. We cannot escape the system the world is living in at this time. We cannot get pure, or self-righteous, or use our spirituality to remove ourselves from the mess we are in. We can only consider our actions within the circle of reciprocity.

This is not a New Age concept. In 1623, in his *Devotions Upon Emergent Occasions*, John Donne wrote his famous soliloquy: "No man is an island, entire of itself; every man is a piece of the continent, a part of the main; if a clod be washed away by the sea, Europe is the less...." He understood. And somewhere inside ourselves I believe we understand. It's just hard to see this reality in our own culture where so much stuff puts us constantly to sleep.

So on a recent trip to Africa I practiced noticing with new eyes. I noticed that people were living side by side in what we would call great wealth and what we would call stark poverty. The wealthy members of the community had many resources and stockpiled goods, just as we do in America, but where the flow of these goods stopped was much more obvious. The goods stopped at the color line. The goods stopped at the neighborhood line. The goods stopped at the economic line. I could wander a shopping mall that was like any mall in the Western world, with the goods priced according to Western standards of living. But outside, at the edge of town, at the edge of the squatter villages, the markets were completely different. Here people sold crafts they had made themselves or bartered from other tribes. Money that would pay for one dinner in the city could buy a family's month supply of cornmeal in the village. In these conditions, to ask — What do I really need? What do I have to offer? — brought fresh insight and awareness. And discomfort to my status quo.

While I pondered these questions, a woman told me with quiet dignity, "We are happy to be poor in Africa, that we might teach the world how to be rich in spirit. Despite our painful history, we are attempting to bring our society back together in a way that honors all those who are here as essential members of the community." She gestured at the razor wire surrounding an opulent property. She gestured at the cardboard and tin shacks and the shared, open cooking fires.

"It is taking too long. Some people are angry. Some people are afraid. Nevertheless, the experiment continues, and we are all in it — and you are in it with us, even though you are thousands of miles away. What are you going to do when you go home?"

At home I am going to stay awake and uncomfortable so that I can think. Not that I know how to solve this dilemma — it being the crisis of the modern age — but I can at least contribute my willingness to be aware. I might, for example, turn to the woman next to me in the grocery store and ask her, "Do you ever wonder how these bananas got here in the middle of winter in a land where they don't grow? Do you wonder whether someone sends the children of the banana pickers apples from the state of Washington in exchange for this gift? Do you think we can do anything to change how so much food comes here, while so little food is left there?" If we question, if we talk with each other, if we hold the ambivalence and donate our concerns from heart to heart, we will eventually act. We will dance with the reciprocity.

And so I find myself out on the balcony again, standing in a misty spring morning with the sights and sounds and smells of Africa still resonating in my jet-lagged body and heart. Some old understanding is stirred in me by my return to a familiar day.

I watch the rain gently fall. I notice the fog accumulate and lift over Puget Sound. I feel the moisture on my skin and how all the molecules of water floating in my body seem to join in this mysterious cycle of transformation. Around me water evaporates, rises as vapor and makes clouds, turns again to rain and falls from the sky. Somewhere in my brain a long-forgotten fifth-grade science project comes to life. I see what the world is doing: I see the unavoidable reciprocity.

The total balance of free water on the planet has been fairly constant since the Precambrian Age, 570 million years ago. That is our supply. That is what we have to trade with in the flow. Life as we know it depends on the relatively stable distribution and redistribution of water between the land, the ocean, and the atmosphere. I can see the cycle of water in a way I cannot see the cycle of energy. I can see how I use water in ways I cannot see how I use energy. I get up and shower, make tea or coffee, notice the weather, water the lawn, buy bottled water at the convenience store, flush the toilet and wash my hands, wash my clothes, and never give that old science diagram of the water cycle a thought. It's harder to understand how the energy cycle moves through all these activities, though I am learning.

I see that we move water, cherish water, waste water, endure dramatic climate changes over which we have no sense of control, but no one is manufacturing more water. I am beginning to see that we also move energy, waste energy, cherish energy, endure dramatic shifts in energy over which we have little sense of control, and that a new conversation about asking for what we need and offering what we can is possible between us all.

I hold my palms out to the rain: I see how I am standing in a life where everything is living in reciprocal relationship with everything else. I see a life where every action creates a corresponding reaction, whether or not I can perceive it or choose to be aware of it.

This is reality. I kiss the rain.

Love the Folks in Front of You

They are my neighbors
I know their name
It s on their mailbox
Yeah, but just the same
I am their neighbor, too,
We say hello
But there is so much more
I want them to know.

Someone lives next door to you
Their feelings do not show
And you can t tell by how they look
What they do or do not know
Chances are that underneath
The wave and the hello
There lives someone that
You might want to know.

Tina Lear, Hello

To love the folks in front of us asks us to look for the good in other people, even if we don't think it's there. We already know how to find friends, how to follow the spark of attraction that causes us to look up, return someone's smile, meet their gaze, and begin to see affinities in each other. This whisper is a commitment to practice seeking that spark when it isn't obvious.

In our speeding, mobile society we have become lazy about love. We have developed a habit of shopping for other people as though we are picking through piles of goods until something strikes our fancy. We leave a clutter of overturned and rejected items in our wake that we expect someone else to put back on the shelf. We have developed a habit of assessing people's worth based on what they might provide us. Unfortunately, most of us know how to walk into a room, peruse the crowd, and determine in seconds whether or not we think anyone present is worth talking to. This is a harsh objectification of our humanity. To love the folks in front of us is a challenge to drop our judgments, and to become curious instead. To love the folks in front of us challenges us to reveal ourselves to one another, to look at the ways we need each other.

There are billions of people on the planet for a reason: if we were meant to be a solitary species, there'd just be one of us. We can walk this peopled path of life establishing relationships that are abusive, manipulative, and objectifying, or we can walk our path establishing relationships of mutuality that are conscientious, co-serving, and respectful of each other's humanity.

Day by day, loving the folks in front of us consists of little moments of connection that build understanding of who we are. These connections become tiny islands of trust that accumulate one action at a time. Our hearts change toward each other, though we may not even remember why or how this came about. We develop a sense of belonging — to our communities, churches, workplaces, groups. We feel at home somewhere.

Our sense of belonging is based on our ability to move around in the company of people who are basically well intentioned and dependable, and who acknowledge our own good intention and dependability in return. Sometimes recognizing each other is easy, but often it's hard work. We can choose compatible friends and lovers, but there remain the long journeys we make with the people we "can't get away from" — and these are often the folks in front of us.

I live on the south end of a long, serpentine island just north of Seattle, Washington, with about twenty thousand other people who reside along beaches or tucked in woods or who congregate in numerous small neighborhoods around unincorporated towns and shopping areas. Four earthquake fault lines run underneath my part of the island, and on a clear day from the high ridge hiking trail at Ebey's Landing, I can see three volcanoes strung along the nearby mountain range. Like a gray haze on the horizon, the blown-off summit of Mount Saint Helens far to the south is a reminder that everything changes. Snowcapped and serene, Mount Rainier dwarfs the Seattle skyline like a huge hovering spacecraft. Her implacable grace hides geologic activity that is studied by scientists from all over the world. To the north, Mount Baker shimmers under year-round glaciers, tolerating skiers on her flanks all winter, and hikers probing their way around ice crevasses between summer storms.

It is a very real possibility that in our lifetimes here, my neighbors and I will need each other's help, cooperation, and collective preparedness to get through a major disaster. This is an island, after all. When I stare into the beauty of this place, I know it is impermanent. And I know it is imperative that I love the folks in front of me. Now.

Every winter, stormy winds of more than 70 MPH pelt the island and knock out power, anywhere from a few hours to a few days. Despite the increasing number of generators that hum in the woods, we occasionally get to practice living together in a pretty basic way. On such a winter day not long ago, the power had been out for several hours and our city friends were finishing a visit by candlelight when there was a knock at the door. I opened it and a shadowed figure said cheerfully, "Hi, it's your neighbor." I couldn't see his face, but the voice was familiar.

"I'm going to every house where someone appears to be home," he said, "to warn folks that a power line has fallen over the road at the entrance to the neighborhood. I don't think anyone should drive over it, but if they cut through my driveway and rough it over the field behind my house they can get in or out."

"Come in," I said. "We have the list for the telephone tree. There are flares in my trunk." Within a few minutes, everyone was safely informed, the power company alerted, and a roadblock set up until we could determine the danger. Five years of neighborliness worked like a charm. This night made it clear that when we need help, we'd better be in good-hearted relationship with the folks within shouting distance.

There's a folksy saying, "If you don't think one individual can make a difference, you've never spent the night in a tent with a mosquito." The same axiom is true about human beings. Who we are and how we behave has tremendous impact on the quality of daily life we create around ourselves. One person's courage to change the conversation from sports and weather to shared concerns of the heart can transform communication in a neighborhood, or committee, or office staff.

We have a deeply ingrained mythology that our family ties are most significant, but here in a little cluster of twenty homes between the woods and cliff, we better practice loving the folks in front of us. My mother lives in British Columbia, my father lives in Maryland, my brothers are in Alaska and Minnesota, my sister is in Wisconsin, and the families of my neighbors are spread just as far and wide. When the tree falls over the driveway, when I wake in the night and hear a strange noise, when the girl at the end of the road skins her knee in front of my house — we need to know each other. And when my mother can't carry a heavy box into her apartment she needs to know a fifty-year-old in her building. And my brothers need to shovel out winter driveways with their neighbors. And my sister needs to have the phone number of where the mommy next door goes to work when the little neighbor girls traipse across the yard for help.

When we moved into this neighborhood, the neighbors who were already here watched to see how we would fit. They nodded and went on their ways. Neighborliness takes a while. We spent the first several years saying hello at the mailboxes, asking, "How are you?" and staying long enough to hear the answer. We helped establish a community workday, encouraged the reinstatement of the annual picnic, and served on the water board. That's how neighborhoods are largely defined on this island: who shares water. Sharing water links us to much of the faraway world and much of human history, in which who gathered around the well has served as a basic definition of community. For many people, who gathers at the well has become who gathers around the office water cooler and the neighbors with whom we spend our waking time are our working colleagues.

And what a wake-up it is to *have* to relate with people who are not selected friends. We may not agree on politics or religion; we may not be social intimates; but sharing a resource that we need in order to live — whether it's water or work — invites us to see that we need each other to live well. Not because someday we might be eating canned beans on the corner lot after an earthquake or company layoff, but because we are each other's people. Our quirks and sensitivities instruct each other exactly because we have not chosen each other.

This is true in apartment buildings, city blocks, workplaces, worship places, businesses, corporations, community and civic organizations. We constantly find ourselves in human clusters where something other than interpersonal affinity has grouped us together. There is always somebody who turns out to be a surprise connection of heart, and there is always somebody, like a cocklebur, ruining the Kiwanis Club meetings, or domineering the Parent Teacher Association, or causing havoc on the work team. And this person provides an opportunity to love the one in front of us who at first seems the least likely to become a friend.

When we moved into this neighborhood, here's what people saw: two midlife white women with two Asian teenagers setting up residence, running a little seminar and adventure business out of a converted shed in the backyard. Within a year we constructed a strawbale house on the back of the lot, a hideaway with a balcony, my desk with a view.

It took months for the man across the street to say hello in response to our greetings. Maybe he was uncomfortable, or maybe he was just shy. Maybe he has long forgotten, for now he and his wife are our closest connections in the neighborhood. We have created a friendship around house and lawn care, love of dogs, and watering each other's gardens when one or the other household is gone on vacation. We have spent dozens of hours standing in our driveways looking for what might connect us, instead of what might separate us.

As a society, we are only a generation or two removed from communities where the network of extended family and neighborhood held people in place. If a kid got in trouble with the shopkeeper, he was lectured soundly, "I know your daddy, I know your uncle, I know your gramma, and your cousins. I'm keeping my eye on you, so you better be good!" People's behavior was held in a social net where accountability was reinforced from the outside. Without that social net, we are called to accountability that is generated from inside. In a society of mass mobility and depersonalization our actions are no longer "policed" by local networks of extended relationship.

While our loss of place has many social consequences, I believe the shift in accountability from outside us to inside us is an evolutionary leap. Loving the folks in front of us is a spiritual practice we do on behalf of our own growth and on behalf of the healing needed all around us.

As we become people who no longer live in the places we come from, which is true now in many parts of the world, we need to replace the sense of place with a willingness to communicate. Perhaps this need accounts for the rising interest in personal story. In the past fifty years in North America and Europe, we have become a society fascinated by story: our own stories, and each other's stories. The media has trivialized this into a cult of gossip and televised revelations by strangers, but the underlying desire for story is genuine. An entire literary genre of memoir has emerged and hundreds of group processes and communication techniques have been designed that help us elicit stories from each other.

So, here we are:

We didn't grow up together. My people don't know your people. And your people don't know my people. Our diversity may be obvious or subtle.

We are brought together without a sense of choice, for reasons we may not understand, often in structures we did not create.

We may share only a narrow band of commonality that has been decided by someone else — to work on the same project, to sit in the same pew, to serve on the same committee. The rest is up to us.

Who are you? And what of who I am will I share with you?

If we share little or nothing of ourselves with each other, we will have little or no relationship. The more we share — that is, the more we have the courage and confidence to reveal ourselves appropriately in the company of strangers — the greater the potential for creating a new social net based on communication.

We may never be best friends, but we can discover compassion for all the history and decisions that go into making the person in front of us who he or she is today. Knowing a person's story softens our reactivity and judgment of each other. Less reactivity equals more tolerance. Less judgment equals more peace. Loving the folks in front of us is a practice that lowers our blood pressure, teaches us to not take things personally, and helps us keep our hearts open rather than slammed shut. It supports good physical, mental, emotional, and spiritual health. And maybe, as we practice on each other, we will develop corresponding understanding and compassion for ourselves.

The stories I'm talking about are the ones beneath the anecdotes. Anecdotes build an initial social fabric, but story builds a sustaining connection.

One year, at the annual neighborhood picnic, we talked about moments in our lives when we had received help from strangers (anecdote). Then we talked about what kind of help we might provide each other (story). The content may be similar, but the vulnerability is usually different.

Making this shift to story can begin with verbal

playfulness. On a committee that seemed bored with its meetings, people wrote down something about themselves they didn't think anyone else knew, put it in a hat, and we all drew out a slip. I pulled the statement, "I used to be a professional race car driver," and looked around the room trying to guess. Then that person elaborated on his story.

At the beginning of a training program for a new work team each person wrote down one question they'd be willing to answer during the week. Some were silly ("If you could be any animal on this team, what would you be and why?"), some were serious ("When did this organization first inspire you and when did it first disappoint you?"). A person always had the right to pass if a topic touched something in them they didn't want to share. As the week progressed, the stories deepened as we came to trust each other.

To hear each other's stories requires time, attention, and an environment of mutual listening. These are precious gifts. One of the most profound ways to share stories is in a council, or circle. When we sit together in a circle we remember how we come from peoples who gathered at the same well, who sat at the same campfires, who depended on oral tradition to remind themselves of who they were.

Somewhere in our minds and bodies *circle* creates a link between our current selves and common ancient sources. A circle is conversation with added pieces of structure that create an interpersonal and spiritual container for whatever stories and issues are shared. This structure often includes a sense of center — putting something down that reminds a group why it is together, like the time we held a water association meeting and put a pitcher of our water on the coffee table along with the latest water quality reports. It may include use of a talking piece, so that only one person speaks at a time, like the committee meeting where three people wanted to talk at the same time. I tossed a pen to one and suggested he speak first and then pass the pen around so we all could comment. And sometimes, especially if the conversation may be emotional or difficult, or just to signal that we share common understandings of respect, it's helpful to articulate a few agreements. Like confidentiality, or assuming good intent, or not taking phone calls in the middle of listening to each other.

Many times the opportunity to create a sense of being in circle happens spontaneously. If we trust ourselves to call in this container for our stories, the quality of what we share will deepen. At my father's eightieth birthday party, when the spouses and grandkids had gone bowling, we four siblings had the chance to reflect with our dad on our relationship over the years. I lit a candle that happened to be sitting on the coffee table, and felt the invocation of the fire. None of us stopped to remark on this gesture; it just helped us go somewhere deeper in our communication.

In the early 1990s, my partner, Ann Linnea, and I developed a council structure called PeerSpirit circling. For over a decade we have been using the circle in our personal lives and introducing council practices into community organizations, corporations, churches and other religious institutions, government agencies, university faculties, and schools. These are all places that often challenge people to find that spark of affinity in the folks with whom they are connected. Bringing the circle into these settings fosters a unique quality of conversation that only occurs when the circle is invoked. Especially in groups where affinity may not be obvious, center, agreements, and purpose provide enough sense of commonality to elicit stories that increase our understanding and acceptance. The use of circle ties what we are doing now to a tradition of appropriate rituals that help us remember how to be wise, compassionate, and forgiving as we face a common concern, goal, or experience.

My friends are accustomed to having both social time and council time when we hang out together. There is, in many of our gatherings, a moment when we shift from the free-for-all of catching up to the formality of sitting down in circle. We put something in the center space between us that reminds us to speak intentionally, listen attentively, and tend to one another's well-being as we reveal our stories.

I doubt that my neighbors would initially be comfortable with such formality, despite its benefits, but I have held meetings with a symbol of our purpose in the center and asked everyone to check in with their own agenda items before starting general discussion.

At the graduation party for a friend's daughter, the girl's parents called everyone into a circle on the lawn in the middle of the open house and set a bouquet of flowers in our midst. People were invited to speak memories, appreciations, and wishes for Amy. This circle was the heart of the gathering, a conversation in which the girl and her family could hear the testimonies of community support as Amy ventures with blessings from the place where she has grown.

It is through taking such incremental risks to see each other freshly and hear each other's stories anew, that we learn to reclaim small units of community and affinity. We are remaking what we need out of what we have. This is good and ancient work. And as I acknowledge in my book *Calling the Circle:*

"It has always been scary
to step into the circle of firelight,
to show up in the company of strangers,
to ask for entrance or to offer it. Our hearts race —
Will we have the courage to see each other?
Will we have the courage to see the world?
The risks we take in the twenty-first century
are based on risks human beings took
thousands of years ago.
We are not different from our ancestors,
they are still here, coded inside us.
They are, I believe,
cheering us on."

❧ Return to the World

When two creatures meet,
as naturally as lake lapping against shore,
or river flowing into sea,
there is a melding, a magic that transcends the everyday.
I felt myself drawn forward into understanding
Mystery and Higher Purpose.
I felt myself anointed and belonging.
I didn't know what was about to happen to me
in the human community toward which I resolutely aimed,
but now I knew I had a community that had claimed me.
She-Who-Was-Afraid had been changed by this journey,
had become Sister-To-Otter.
Had become Woman-At-Home-In-The-Wild.

Ann Linnea, Deep Water Passage

Return to the world means return to the *real* world. Return to the world of the body, the senses, the world of Nature. The preamble to my daily prayer begins by honoring the world. "Creator of All," I whisper into the morning air, "thank you for this day. Thank you for the sun that rises and sets, for the wind that blows, the rain that falls. Thank you for the air that I breathe, the food that I eat, and the sustenance that You provide. *May all that I do today contribute to the healing of the world, and may my heart be open enough to allow the world to contribute to my healing.*" Letting the earth heal us, and devoting ourselves to healing the earth — now there's a reciprocal relationship worth tending.

These whispers work in a circular fashion. We start by calming ourselves, seeking peace of mind by taking in breath. And what is breath? Nature. Nature's gift: the exhalation of trees. As long as we are alive, the journey of spirituality always returns us to the body: we are of the earth.

A few springtimes ago, I attended a conference in a downtown hotel in a big American city. About three thousand other participants and I were talking about bringing spirituality into the workplace. The first morning at breakfast I noticed a plant had been placed at the end of the buffet table to add a little greenery. But two of its leaves were roasting in the sterno can under the scrambled eggs. Nobody seemed to notice or care. I moved the leaves, got my scrambled eggs.

The next day the plant had been placed in exactly the same position, its two withered leaves turned to the wall, and two new leaves now sacrificed to the sterno fires. I moved it again while the waiter eyed me suspiciously. "It's a living thing," I said to him, "— the plant." I was dressed in a two-piece pantsuit, wearing my presenter badge, looking about as "normal" as I ever do and didn't want to push him too far here. "I mean, what if while you were serving breakfast," I ventured on, "you had two fingers stuck in the flame and couldn't move or even yelp...."

"Did you want bacon with that, ma'am?" It was the only thing he was programmed to say.

In the past few centuries of industrialization and urbanization — leading to our current technostructure — we have strayed so far from home we have almost no idea what Nature is. The closest we get to comprehension is to say we ought to realign our lives with Nature, as though this were an option. As though we were separate. As though we have dominion over the miraculous biosphere that designed us from the molecule up.

I ate the tasteless eggs, chewed on a rubbery bagel, and went outside to walk among the throngs of rushing people weaving around the potted trees on their ways to work. We cannot bring spirituality into the workplace, or anywhere else, without bringing Nature in.

Yet Nature is no longer real to millions and millions of people in the West. We have stopped believing somehow that we live in Nature, and see it instead as an inconvenience represented by the day's weather, while we hustle about in our temperature-controlled capsules, breathing recycled air. Many of us think of real Nature as a vacation destination, or a romanticized oddity on the Discovery Channel — not occurring where we live.

There is no other world: Nature is the world. And we are Nature — in it, of it, and totally linked with its fate. Isn't it obvious by now? what we do to the earth we are doing to ourselves: what we do to ourselves we are doing to the earth. Every whisper leads to this one, our invitation home.

Remember... how to spend an hour just walking around a block. How to jump in piles of autumn leaves. How to lick snowflakes off a mitten. How to slip out of school clothes and into jeans, then run off to a nearby creek to catch tadpoles, or make forts in tall grass, or play 'til summer dusk when the fireflies are coming out. Remember hiding out in a patch of woods, enthralled with fantasies of Nature spirits. Remember the heat of city evenings rising up the shaft of fire escapes and the pigeons swirling off an apartment roof. Remember when the peregrine falcons nested on skyscrapers and the people in suits paused to watch a spiral of winged freedom circling high over city intersections. Remember...

We can start to rejoin our lives with Nature by doing what Nature does. Nature moves in cycles of sprouting, growth, harvest, rest. When I am standing on my balcony, Nature invites me to notice which season it is in, and which season I am in. The long days of summer, when the birds sing me awake before 5 A.M., have a different productivity to them than the short days of winter when the mountains glow with sunset at 4:30 in the afternoon. So summer is a good time to get more done; winter is a good time to get more rest. My body wants to follow this cycle: how can I honor my body?

Nature gives abundantly, in a pattern where everything is used and useful and connected. We can notice this pattern around us and weave earth-tending into our everyday lives. We can go for a walk and pick up the trash. We can plant something. Even one gera-nium will teach us. We can practice watching the phases of the moon — for no special reason, except that it will get us to look up at the sky. It will get us to notice how much of the sky we can or cannot see from where we live. We can educate ourselves about the plants and animals that live around us. They are not aliens or adversaries, just co-inhabitants. Before I attempt to introduce something new or get rid of something already present I ought to first understand where it sits in the food chain, how it fits in the pat-tern, and what I might be disrupting.

We can retrieve the children parked in front of the televisions and computer monitors and take them back outdoors. To raise a generation for whom the simu-lated world is more real than the real world is very dangerous. When I was a child my greatest escape was into Nature. Now children hunker indoors as though to escape from Nature.

Though he has now returned to his interest in wild adventures, I remember a magnificent full eclipse of the moon a few years ago when I tried to get my step-son outside to watch it with me. "I already know about it," he informed me. "They interrupted programming

— it's on TV." This was not meant as an antagonistic exchange, and it came out of the mouth of a young man whose mother had first taken him trekking in the wilderness before he could walk.

"No," I told him. "The moon is *not* on TV; it's at the end of the block, with a clear shot of the universe. TV is a picture."

We are in huge trouble if we have neglected to teach our children to love the world. We are in huge trouble if we ourselves have neglected to love the world — and it certainly seems that we have.

In his book *The Healing Wisdom of Africa*, Dagara tribal teacher Malidoma Somé reminds us:

[Y]ou have to walk into Nature with your emotional self, not with your intellectual self. You need to open wide your heart so that you can become moist and drink deeply from the emotional echoes that you receive from the frown of a gnarled tree or the twist of a branch. Seen in this way, Nature, the dwelling place of the ancestral spirits, is a vast field of grief. I say this because every harmful thing done to the earth is registered in Nature. Nature is the place where the real work of healing takes place slowly and gradually. This is because Nature cannot ignore the wounds that humans inflict on one another or on her.

What I really know about healing has come from Nature itself. This is not book learning; this is experience. Nature is the only thing big enough to hold us in our moments of greatest pain and joy. Instinctively we go outside, run from the city streets to the wilderness edge, wherever we can find it. We take home our elation and our broken hearts to the clay from which we come.

On a vision quest in southeast Alaska several summers ago, I had the opportunity to spend a week with the planet, just Her and me and a few friendly souls scattered in the coastal rain forest a thousand miles north of my home island. Once a year our guide, David, brings people to a tiny unnamed bay usually inhabited only by bears and eagles, seals, dolphins, and humpback whales. Here the only footprints of humankind were the ones this little troop of seekers made ourselves. And so I could see my impact upon the environment. I noticed the crushed moss, the bent grasses, the broken clusters of barnacle my clumsy feet made on an absolutely pristine land.

Here was ground that had never been hurt: not logged or fished or cultivated. The place was pure and free. I put up my tent, silently asking for permission to tie a rope to trees, or to drive a stake into the forest floor, because I could see the scar on the bark, see the hole in the moss. In the evening's long twilight I peered into trembling shadows — requesting clearance from the unseen bears. I pumped water the color of cola through my filter and drank nutrients straight from the roots of cedar, hemlock, and Sitka spruce. It was rainy and cold, and I crawled into my mummy bag wearing every article of clothing I had along except my boots and rain suit. There was no one else in sight. I kept the canister of pepper gas, known fondly in these parts as bear spray, tucked under my pillow. I lay down in the dusk of summer solstice in the far north. "Okay, I'm here," I whispered. "I am here to love the world."

And all that week the world forgave me and loved me back. My most profound teacher will be the place itself. Will be the chance to live on the planet, in the epidermal layer of the earth's energetic skin. That first night, I learned the most important part of the quest would be the amount of time I spent within three feet of the ground.

Whenever we sit or lie directly on the ground, we put our bodies inside this "skin." How many times I have finally laid down in the grass of my backyard, or nestled in the warm packed sand of the beach and wondered how different the world would be if grownups spent more time in this position. What if we conducted business while making daisy chains, or had conference calls while weeding flowerbeds?

So I lie in my tent. My ears strain into the white noise of rainy forest listening for bear's breath. I pray for protection and wonder why I think I deserve it. I feel nervous and out of place in the midst of so much impersonal aliveness. I take three breaths: one to let go, one to be here, one to ask now what? I am a woman crossing into the twenty-first century; I do not know what is happening to me. I choose to trust the world. I am the great-great-great-great-granddaughter of some unknown Celtic shaman, and that is the lineage I draw out of my cells.

I am not exactly awake, but not exactly asleep. After awhile, it feels as though the earth begins to cradle me and I feel plugged into a flow that surges through me all night long. I maintain peace of mind while the wild world courses through my body, cleansing civilization out of my bones. Sometime before dawn I seem to see deep into the forest, where there sits a rise of cliff maybe fifty feet high — a mossy rock wall with a stream shooting out of a crevice. I understand this vision is a portal to the wholeness of the world. I understand this portal is a possibility waiting for me to understand how to enter.

The next morning we ten seekers huddle under quilts in the community tent listening to the drip, drip, drip of the incessant rain, alternating chants and silence as we learn how to live with the real world. I remember the question I am carrying: how do I move at the pace of guidance, no matter what pace the world is asking me to move? I look around and begin to see the pace of Nature. Here is my chance to sit with this question in a council of trees and boulders, in the company of hummingbirds and eagles. Maybe the real world will show me how to return to real pace.

Of course I have come here with a certainty of purpose. This is a vision quest, after all, and I want to make good use of my time. I have an intention statement taped inside my journal cover and a list of questions to ask God about the next portion of my journey. This list buzzes in my mind like no-see-ums buzz through the mesh of the tent. We are chanting lines of song from various traditions: words in English, Latin, Sanskrit. We pass a talking stone around the circle and listen to each other's dreams. I am impatient for insight, and not particularly interested in the rambling stories of my neighbors.

At the beginning of this retreat there is not a lot of spiritual territory open in me. I begin to realize how angry I am, how much my mind is ranting instead of chanting. I am mad at life for not meeting my expectations. I am mad at my distraction and busyness. I am mad at what is happening or not happening in our work. I am mad at myself for being dispirited and inattentive to love. I am mad at myself for being such a spiritual fool, wasting so much time being in my head instead of in my life.

"The mind is clever," David whispers, "but the heart is truly intelligent." As the days pass, my mind finally gives up its determination to make sure certainty happens and drifts off to meander the rainy woods. "The mind plans and plans how to get better, but things don't really get better until the heart actually shifts." My heart begins listening to the world.

At night, all night, the earth plugs me into itself and I lie prone and vibrating on the forest floor. What I have long believed was possible, I am now experiencing. Finally, finally, I have grown up enough to let divine sensation have its way with me again. Finally, finally, I become willing to simply lie down on the earth and cry for my vision. Tears leak from my eyes. I am not wailing, not whining, not caught up in my little faraway dramas. I am raining — the forest and I — raining. This gentle act brings forth help. I surrender to surprises.

After three days of community routine, I am ready to leave the group and head off into solo time. I ask for what I need and am released to make my way out of the forest and to the rocky point that overlooks the sea. I offer what I can, a blessing to Sally, a hug for Rick, an extra energy bar for C.J. I restore my first campsite to its pristine condition as much as I can and load up my backpack, as I'll have to re-establish my tent at the edge of the world. I find David and turn in my canister of bear spray. He looks surprised. "I can't say I trust the world and go out there 'armed for bear.'" I tell him, "I want to take my place as a creature among creatures.

Four hours later, I am perched in the tiniest clearing at the edge of a hundred-foot drop to the sea. My only neighbors are eagles nesting in the next tree. It's still raining. I'm fasting on tree-filtered water. I have a small camp stove and I'm heating water to put in my water bottle and roll up in a sock to warm my toes at the bottom of the sleeping bag. I am singing a simple chant of "Hal-le-lu-jah" based on the sweetly descending and ascending notes of Pachelbel's Canon, over and over, fifteen minutes at a time. It makes the sinus cavities buzz in my head, and the low note buzzes in the firm muscle of my diaphragm. I am writing in my journal. I am thinking of all the journeys that lead to this journey, and all the companionship that leads to this solitude.

The first time I walked in the wilderness with Ann Linnea, she fell to her knees among trees like these. Fell to her knees and tears leapt from her eyes. I sheltered her back, and waited to understand. When she could speak, she spoke for the trees. Here on this precarious point of land, with no others of my kind, I understand what Ann experienced that day. I experience my own ability to expand perception, to let the heart of wildness beat within my human heart. I love the folks in front of me — the trees, the eagles, the salal, the rocks, the sea, a whale.

The word indigenous means "belonging to place." I was born in Montana, the daughter of a Celt and a Scandinavian. On the coattails of their wandering, I lived in five states before I was nine years old. In the decades of my own wandering I have lived in another half dozen places and traveled in two dozen countries. And this is all I want: to understand how to belong, not only to the cities, but also to the land. I want to come home to the earth again.

That night, when I venture out between the tent flaps, the clouds are breaking and stars appear overhead. Is this what I meant, those years ago on the family porch when I prayed to have my full life? Was it here I was heading? To become a half-naked woman peeing in the grass?

I turn around and the portal from the deep woods has followed me here. Shimmers in twilight. Do I have the courage to enter my own dream?

Yes, now I do.

The woman who is my dreaming self rises and bows to the dreaming bear. The bear returns the bow and invites the woman on her back. Woman digs her fingers into the bear's fur thick and tangled with burrs. She feels bear muscles moving in the lope between her legs. She rides confidently as the bear carries her through the underbrush toward the rock wall with its moss, its running stream, the crevice that opens to a cave.

Teacher senses them coming. If anyone finds this wellspring it must be a daughter or son, for only one of her lineage has the map for finding, or even the desire to search. Teacher dips her gourd in the stream, filling it with fresh water to offer the thirsty travelers.

They are here now. But instead of descending from the bear's back, the woman and the bear become one body: womanbear, woman dressed in bearskin, same intense eyes, soft hair. She bows to Teacher. Offers a bowl of berries in exchange for water from the sacred spring. "I am sorry to have been so delayed," she whispers. "In the times I come from, in the places where I have lived, there are many obstacles to believing the dream. But finally I was strong enough to venture out beyond the edges. Thank you for waiting."

"I am not waiting," says Teacher, "I am simply here. You will see what you are capable of seeing, and you will be what you are capable of being." She turns to the woman, and holds out a mirror. "Behold," she says, "and remember who you are."

The womanbear regards her true self. She falls down weeping, laughing, digging her hands into the moss and smelling, tasting, touching the green of the world. A moment of true infinity passes. She utters one word — "Thank you."

When I wake in the morning the sun has come out in southeast Alaska. Snowcapped mountains ring my view and I can see all the way to the curve of the earth, two hundred miles in either direction. And, oh dear God, in this sparkling beauty I return to the world.

There on the farthest horizon sits a tiny black spot that looks like palm trees floating in this northern sea. When I squint through binoculars, I see what must be the tops of firs and hemlock, the island itself below the horizon line, and only these sentinels visible from the perspective of my rock. I look down and see eddylines of current carrying driftwood and kelp and the occasional seal steadily toward this unknown destination. I realize this *is* what is happening: we are all drifting and swimming toward an unknown point that will not be what it seems when we get there. The goodness in us and the world, the badness in us and the world, the tension and the confusion and these moments of astounding grace, all adrift together.

The covenant made with the angel is not about leading an ordinary or extraordinary life in any terms I have understood, but about leading whatever life we have with extraordinary attention to God's call and our response: our call and God's response.

The fir trees that surround my house remind me of their cousins that stand at No-Name Bay. I am connected to the world in ways I will never fully understand. I only know it is morning. I find a place to stand and say these seven whispers for me and for you.

The Seven Whispers

Maintain peace of mind

Move at the pace of guidance

Practice certainty of purpose

Surrender to surprise

Ask for what you need and offer what you can

Love the folks in front of you

Return to the world

Afterword

Thank you for journeying with me through these seven whispers. These phrases currently serve as the core of my own spiritual practice. You are welcome to claim and use them, and even more welcome to adapt them to your journey, and to come up with your own.

Perhaps someday we will meet and discover what we have been whispering into the ear of the Divine, and how our lives have been changed as a result. Meanwhile —

May we be of service
to whatever goodness is trying to happen in the world
in these terrible and wonderful times.

Christina Baldwin
Fall 2001

❧ Chapter Notes

Chapter One
Etty Hillesum, *An Interrupted Life, the Diaries of Etty Hillesum 1941–1943*, Pantheon Books: New York, 1983, translated from the Dutch.

Chapter Two
Gerald May, *Will and Spirit: A Contemplative Psychology*, HarperSanFrancisco: San Francisco, 1982.

Joseph Campbell, with Bill Moyers, *The Power of Myth*, Doubleday: New York, 1988.

Chapter Three
William Wordsworth, "The Ode on Intimations of Immortality from Recollections of Early Childhood," 1803–06.

Chapter Four
Clara Claiborne Park, *The Siege*, Little Brown: Boston, 1982.

Chapter Six
Christina Baldwin, *Calling the Circle: the First and Future Culture*, Bantam: New York, 1998.

Chapter Seven
Malidoma Patrice Somé, *The Healing Wisdom of Africa*, Tarcher/Putnam: New York, 1998.

David LaChapelle, *Navigating the Tides of Change*, New Society Press: Saltspring Island, British Columbia, 2001.

❧ Permissions Acknowledgments

The author and publisher gratefully acknowledge permission to quote and source materials used throughout this book. In some cases short quotes have been used under fair use, and in other cases permission was sought and granted. In either case, we honor the lineage of written wisdom that helps frame this book.

Excerpt from "Healing" from *What Are People For?* by Wendell Berry, copyright © 1990 by Wendell Berry. Reprinted with permission of North Point Press, a division of Farrar, Straus and Giroux, LLC.

"Holy the Firm," by Annie Dillard, copyright © 1977 by Annie Dillard. Reprinted with permission of HarperCollins Publishers, Inc. New York.

Excerpt from *Deep Water Passage: A Spiritual Journey at Mid-life*, Pocketbooks, copyright © 1997 by Ann Linnea. Reprinted with permission of the author.

"Tonight Everyone in the World Is Dreaming the Same Dream," by Susan Litwak from *Voices within the Ark: Modern Jewish Poets*, edited by Howard Schwartz and Anthony Rudolf, copyright © 1980 by Susan Litwak. Reprinted with permission of the author.

"Hello," original song, copyright ©1999 by Tina Lear. Reprinted with permission of the author.

Evelyn Underhill, *Practical Mysticism*, Ariel Press: Columbus, Ohio, from 1914 edition, reprinted with permission of E. P. Dutton.

🌿 Author Acknowledgments

Writing is a rigorous spiritual dance and I am grateful for the companions who danced with me during the time I wrote this book.

Of course there is my agent, Joe Durepos, who took the seven whispers off my email signature line and challenged me to "do something with these." Then there is Jason Gardner at New World Library who purchased an idea, let me run with it, and got excited at the results. What a pleasure to work with an editor who edits and laughs at my stories of writing frenzy. I look forward to getting to know this company as the life of this book continues.

Several circles of writing women listened to these pages and helped me get down to the core material. Thank you to Sheila Belanger, Ann Linnea, Pamela Sampel, Linda Secord, Sandy Smith, Janie Starr, Clare Taylor, Mary Brooks Tyler, Kit Wilson, M. K. Sandford, and Colleen Baldwin. Thank you to the Spiritual Neighbors Circle for prayers and support, especially Roger. Thank you to Claudia Walker for setting the whispers to music and humming a sweet chant in the chambers of my mind. Thank you to Julie Gersten for genius bodywork and neighborliness, and Debbie Dix for holding the PeerSpirit office together during months of writing. Thank you to an incredible community of friends and family, near and far, who help me walk the walk of this life. This includes my parents, Leo Baldwin and Connie McGregor, for imbuing me with a restless spirit, and my brothers, Carl and Eric, and sister, Becky, for welcoming me all these years along their own life paths. And thank you to Ann for being my primary spiritual practice.